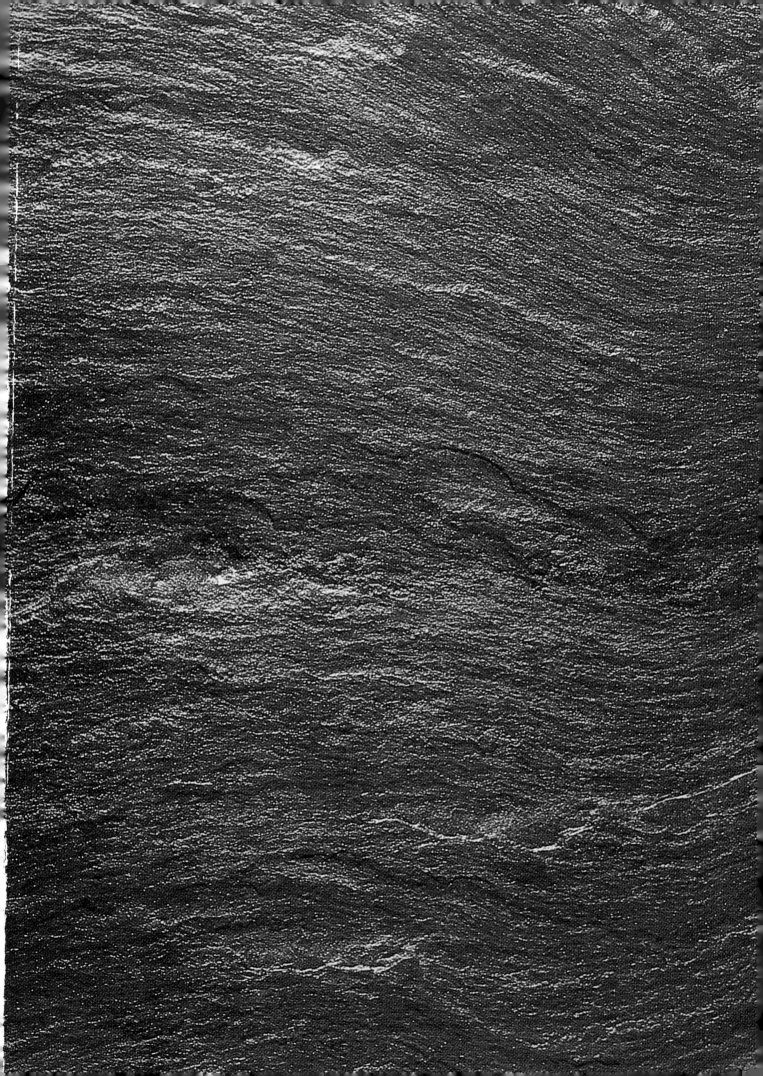

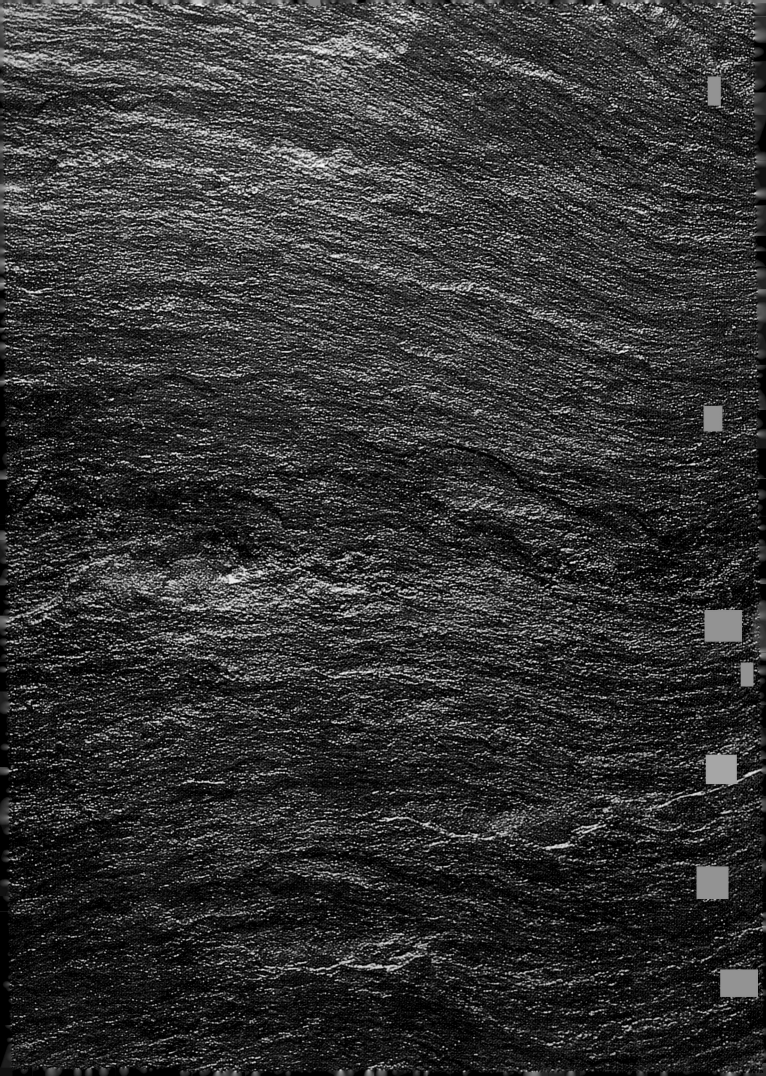

更立西江石壁，截断巫山云雨，高峡出平湖。神女应无恙，当惊世界殊。

毛泽东

夔门天下雄
The Magnificent Kui Gate

序

长江三峡，西起四川奉节县的白帝城，东至湖北省宜昌市的南津关，由瞿塘峡、巫峡、西陵峡组成，全长192公里。这里山显千姿，水呈百态，洞藏神奇，人透古秀，以其雄、险、奇、秀的自然风光，闻名古今，饮誉中外，构成了长江这只交响乐中最为瑰丽的一个乐章。

峡区风光，伟奇深幽，各具风格。瞿塘峡以岩陡谷窄、雄壮险峻著称。峡谷长度虽只8公里，但重岩叠峰，隐天蔽日，船行其间好似"峰与天关接，舟从地窟行"，自有奇险之趣。巫峡以幽深秀丽盛名，它像一条迂回曲折的画廊，呈现出"山塞疑无路，湾回别有天"的迷人景观。巫峡的云最美，唐朝诗人元稹写过"曾经沧海难为水，除却巫山不是云"的名诗。西陵峡是长江三峡中最长一峡，它峡山嵯峨，江流回环，滩多水急。三峡的雄、险、奇、秀的风光，这里都能看到，还有众多的名胜古迹和优美传说，北宋欧阳修曾盛赞"西陵山水天下佳"。

峡区人文，钟灵毓秀，流芳千古。这里孕育出伟大的爱国诗人屈原和民族友好使者王昭君；李白、杜甫、白居易、苏轼、陆游、欧阳修都在这里留下了他们的足迹和佳作。

画册中所展现出来的，不仅是一幅幅精美旖旎的三峡风光，而且还有作者对三峡的那份梦绕魂萦的情感。它不仅是作者的一份真挚情怀，也表达了我们对三峡的未来的美好祝愿。

王重农

1997.9 于武昌水果湖

Preface

The Three-Gorges starts from the White Emperor Town, Fengjie county, Sichuan province in the west, and ends at Nanjing Pass, Yichang City, Hubei province in the east. It consists of such three gorges as Qutang Gorge, Wu Gorge and Xiling Gorge with a distance of192 km. Here, mountains appear various shapes; Waters emerge different forms; Grottos hide mystic power and the inhabitants look simple and honest. It is also famous for its magnificence, precipitousness and elegance.

The picturesque landscapes at Gorge area see both magnificent and mysterious. Qutang Gorge enjoys the reputation of steep cliffs and deep valleys. It is only 8 kms long. Yet, the peaks and rocks pile up. When you sail in it, you seem to enter into a land of "Peaks link to the sky, and boats penetrate through the valley". Wu Gorge is famous for its elegance, which looks like a belt of art gallery. The clouds are the most attractive to which Yuanzhen, a renowned poet in Tang Dynasty, devoted a line. Xiling Gorge is one of the longest part of the Three Gorges. here, it is known as perilous mountains, surging waters and violent rapids. In addition, you can also witness numerous scenic spots and historic interests and beautiful folktales. No wonder Ou Yangxiu in North Song Dynasty praised it as "of the best sceneries Xiling tops".

The culture and tradition are abundant here. This land nourishes such an excellent poetic genius as Quyuan (the patriotic poet) and a talented beauty as Wang Zhaojun. Many great poets as Li Bai, Du Fu, Bai Juyi, Su Shi, Lu You, Ou Yangxiu attrbuted their lyric verses to this land.

What reveals in this Pictorial does not only reflect a gallery of beautiful landscapes in Gorege area but also express the photographers' deeply-rooted emotions. It also embodies the compilers' real feelings as well as their best wishes for the bright future of the Three Gorges.

中国の長江の上流には雄大で、奇麗な大峡谷がある。それは、四川省奉節県の白帝城から、湖北省宜昌市の南津関まで、全長１９２Ｋｍの間、瞿塘峡、巫峡、西陵峡という三つの峡谷からなっているので、長江三峡と呼ばれている。境内には奇峰が連なり、怪石がそびえ、流れの声が響き、雲や霧がまつわりめぐり、まさに山水画のようである。古来,文墨古跡が数多くのこっている。今は世界注目の三峡水利電力プロジェクトの建設中にこの神奇美妙な自然風景を船旅で楽しめるのは最高である。

夔门
Kui Gate

银河九天下，蟠桃与日升
The falling water downs from the sky
And the peach blossoms bright.

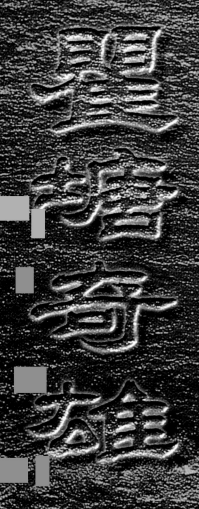

瞿塘峡西起白帝城，东至巫山黛溪镇，全长8公里。瞿塘峡壮观、奇雄、险峻。两岸断崖怪石嶙峋，临江壁立，其高千仞，而江面不足百米，大有"夫当关，万夫莫开"之势。因而故有"夔门"之称。

这里天为山欺峡，水为石放行，这是三峡中距离最短、航道最短、航道最窄，最为峥嵘突兀而又最为气势磅礴的苍桑峡谷。江流至此，澎湃激越，在瞿塘峡峡口形成"万水争门"之奇雄景观。

Magnificent Qutang Gorge

Qutang Gorge starts from White Emperor Town in the west, and ends at Dai Brook Town in the east. It covers a distance of 8 kms. It is famous for its majestic appearance, magnificent scenery and steep cliffs. On the banks lie the grotesque stones and rocks which face the great river. A number of high peaks surround the river, and the river is no more 100 m wide. So in the ancient times, It is an important strategic point, thus enjoying the reputation of "Ghost Gate".

With mountains overshadowing the sky and rocks checking the way of waterflow, it's also the shortest, narrowest, yet the most perilous and torrential of the Three Gorges. The water floods here with the surging waves and forms a grand outlook of "many waters pour the pass" at the mouth of Qutang Gorge.

瞿塘峡は長江三峡の入り口にあたり、白帝城から巫山黛渓鎮まで、全長8ｋｍで、三峡のなかでは一番短いが、両岸は高さ数百メートルの断崖絶壁が聳えて、川幅が１００ｍ足らず、流れは最も急峻であり、最初の難所となり、夔門とも称されている。また、峰は天に繋がり、舟は地底に行くというほどの景観の雄大さで随一である。

子規幽幽啼
夔门秋月冷
Gloomily, gloomily the cuckoo crows,
Cool, cool the autumnmoon is at Kui Pass.

Twilight at Kui Gate

奇峰高万仞，一叶下巴东。
金轮出碧水，丹霞染苍穹。
Peculiar cliffs stand high,
A skiff floats down Badong at ease.
Golden sunshine rises from horizon,
Rainbowlike rays coat the sky.

夔门向晚
Twilight at Kui Gate

夔门晨曦
The Morning of Kui Gate

壁立千仞之上，遥远的　　　High above the thousand peaks,
山峦在向更远处聚合　　　　The remote mountains fly out of reach,
仅有的一幅风景是缄默的　　Only a spot of scenery remains silent.
岩石和岩石下生命的暗流　　The subriver beneath the rocks,
它要和江水一起走出　　　　Flows east, together with the river.
大地峻深的怀抱

奉节
Fengjie county

绝壁铁索寒，纤夫含泪行。
At perilous cliffs the iron-rope seems chill
Boat trackers march on with tear

纤夫索道
The Rope-path on the Cliff for Boat Trackers

峡江信号工
The Signalmen

古栈道
The Ancient Plank Road

据说早在秦朝初年，人们沿大宁河在岩石上凿口插木，铺设竹筒，引卤水煮煎。到汉朝末年已形成全长二百二十华里的栈道。栈道石孔分上下两排，排列整齐，错落有致。

如今，我们望着这千年长栈，凭吊古战场。耳畔似闻兵马萧萧、杀敌怒吼，饶多古思。

It says that as early as Qin Dynasty, people welled holes on the rocks and covered with planks made of bamboo clappers fried by the salt water along Daning River. To the end of Han Dynasty, it formed a 220 li plank path which is classified into two even, regular rows (high and low).

Nowadays, when we stare at the old plank path, visit the old battle-field, we seem to see the spears, daggers and chariot-wheels in our eyes, and hear shouts, cries in our ears.

江峡云霁

The Cloudy Gorge

穿过灵魂的视线，一座古老的　　　An old mountain pauses its steps in my soul's eye,
山峰静止了时间？缓缓　　　　　　Slowly, slowly,
流泻的江水就像我们朝圣的心　　　The flowing river runs eastward in patience,
在隐忍中坚持着的，那是　　　　　like the holy pilgrimages.
风与日光的女儿，一抹轻纱　　　　It is the daughter of wind and sunlight.
透出了它永远淡雅绰约的风骨　　　A ray of mist transparents its ever-lasting glamour and grace

听涛
Listening to the Waves

西汉居摄三年（公元 8 年），据蜀称王的
公孙述在此筑城。因城中一古井每晨常有白
气升腾，其视如"白龙献瑞"，故自称"白帝"，
该城遂名为白帝城。公孙述被灭后，人们在
白帝城修庙，供祀公孙述像，名白帝庙。

During West Han Dynasty(8.B.C), a
military general named Gong Sanshu
crowned himself and began to build city.
In the town centre, a white steam rose
high from an old well resembling a white
dragon presenting luck. So it was called
White Emperor Town, After Gong was
killed, people began to build temple here
to hold his portrait. It was called white
Emperor Temple.

森然白帝庙
The White Emperor Temple

古码头依斗门
The Ancient Dock and Yidou Gate

公元220年，蜀汉皇帝刘备被东吴陆逊火烧连营700里，兵败退守白帝城，病逝永安宫。临终前，将儿子刘禅托付给丞相诸葛亮，历史上称此事为"白帝托孤"。

At 220. B. C, Liubei, the emperor of Shu Kingdom, and his armies were defeated by Lu Xun, a general of Wu Kingdom, who fired Liu's 700 li barracks, so, he retreated and passed away at Yongan Palace. White Emperor Town, Before his death, he entrusted his son to the care of zhuge Liang, the prime minister. In history it's called "Entrusting the son at White Emperor Town".

《刘备托孤》彩塑
Liu Bei entrusting his son to the Care of zhuge
Liang the master mind (colored sulpture)

赤甲晴晖
Sunshine at Red Mail Hill

　　远古时，巴蜀多水患，良田变苍海。大禹决心开峡、引水，多年不成，天庭派神将瞿翁相助。倾刻间，烈火腾然。拦江的一座大山炼成了通红的铁甲(赤甲山)，把临近一座山熔为白盐(白盐山)。禹挥巨斧，峡乃劈开。后人为了纪念大禹和瞿翁，就把雄伟壮丽的峡谷称为"瞿塘峡"。

　　In the ancient times, flood run wild throughout the Bashu land, Fertile fields turn into a sea of waters, Dayu (the King) was determined to release the floodwater and open a channel but without success. The Heaven was moved by his efforts, so sent a general named Qu Weng for help. Instantly, a fire broke out, smelting a mountain blocking the way into a burning mail and a neighouring mountain into a salty one. So Dayu splited the mountain with a huge axe and the waterway was formed. The later generations naturally named this magnificent gorge as "Qutang Gorge" in honor of them.

巫峡 位居 三峡之中部，西起四川巫山大宁河口，东至湖北巴东官渡口，全长42公里。

巫峡大部分是由石灰岩构成。滴水穿石，岩体呈现出无数深邃的沟壑和陡峭的山壁。沟愈深，山峰愈显得高峻俊美；峰愈高，沟壑愈显得幽深寂静。俯瞰：峡江似练，翠峰如簇，巫山十二峰郁郁葱葱，青幽奇画。唐代诗人刘禹锡曾留下"巫山十二郁苍苍，片石亭亭号女郎"的诗句。而巫山云雾尤为一绝，正所谓"除却巫山不是云"。峡谷内云蒸雾蔚，随处可见。每一座山峰、每一斗流水都流传着许多动人的传说。

巫峡是三峡中较长而又整齐的一段，故而又称之为"大峡"。

Misty Wu Gorge

Wu Gorge is located in the middle of the Three Gorges. It starts from the mouth of Daning River of Wushan County, Sichuan in the west, and ends at Guandu pass of Badong County, Hubei in the east. It's 42 km long.

It is mainly composed of lime stones. Constant water corrosion penetrates the rocks so that there form many deep gullies and steep cliffs on the surface. The more deep the gullies are , the more beautiful the cliffs are; the more high the mountains are, the more serene and tranquil the gullies seem. looking down, the river looks like a belt, the mountains crowd together. The Twelve Peaks seem a land of green and imagination . No wonder the great poet Liu Yuxi described it as "The Twelve peaks shrouded with dark green, The upright stones invite the fairy queen". Morever, Mt. Wu's mists and clouds are most attractnie.

The clouds surge and mists rise here and there among the valley. In addition, many touching tales and legends originate from the mountains and rivers here.

Wu Gorge is the longest and most even part of the Three Gorges, and enoys the reputation of "Main Gorge".

四川省大寧河口から湖北省巴東の官渡口まで全長四十二ｋｍの間は巫峡である。緩やかな流れの両側には神女峰をはじめ、１２の美しい峰が次々現れ、飽きることはない。

碧霄神女
Goddess in Mists

神女远眺
Goddess Staring Far

巫峡登龙峰　Dragon-Climbing Peak

巫峡横石　Crossing Stone of Wu Gorge

川江沉寂
Tranquil Chuan River

Endless clouds drift, peaceful and ease,
at pavilion beside river and hill they cease.

云雨
Clouds and Rains

片片飞来静又闲，楼头江上复山前。
Endless clouds drift, peaceful and ease,
at pavilion beside river and hill they cease.

峡江春早　**Early Spring**

若教春有意，惟遣一枝芳。
If spring flowers blossom,
Can spring be far away?

风急天高猿啸哀，渚清沙白鸟飞回。
无边落木萧萧下，不尽长江滚滚来。

The violent wind, the high sky,
and the monkeys' sad adieus,
Birds fly fro and to the clean, sandy isles.
Thousands of rafts rush down so swift,
To the lower reach, the endless Yangtze River drift.

幽深的巫峡
The Gloomy Wu Gorge

山桃花红满山头，蜀江春水拍山流。
The mountains are shrouded with
peach flowers and butterflies,
And spring water of Shu River
flows and towers in the pure skies.

巫峡碚石
Bei Stone at Wu Gorge

山桃花红满山头，蜀江春水拍山流。
The mountains are shrouded with
peach flowers and butterflies,
And spring water of Shu River
flows and towers in the pure skies.

神女情长天地间，望君千载眼皆穿。
江涛难洗相思苦，云涌香魂飘万山。
The Goddess wanders between the heaven and
earthly land ;
Gazing at you for thousand years with tears
down my hand ,
The waves fail to throw away my lovesickness,
And the souls glimpse thousand hills with the
turbulent cloud.

巫峡集仙峰
Fairies-gathering Peak

是峡风还是云彩
把这古典的峰峦打开
不再去唱忧伤的歌谣
希望已朝我们走来
Is it the wind or cloud
which open the beautiful height.
I don't chant a melancholy tone,
And my mood is fine.

落晖
The Sunset Glow

这样的日暮黄昏．
我看到的是流水鼓动的大地的弦．

峭壁如林　The Steep Cliffs

"峭壁如林"，乃山水长年流淌，滴水穿石所致的特殊景观。
The steep cliffs are formed by the constant waterdrops
penetrating throught the rocks, thus displaying a peculiar view.

巫山与天近，
烟蒙逸轻盈。
此中襄王梦，
梦得神女灵。
神女去已久，
白云空冥冥。
唯有大江意，
苍茫直奔东。

Mt. Wu meets the sky,
The mists fly far and high,
Once King Xiang had a dream,
The Goddess bathing in a stream.
Her majesty has gone away,
The pure cloud floats on its way.
Only the Great River is haste,
Flows eastward with no rest.

幽深的巫峡
The Gloomy Wu Gorge

雪霁

江水迢迢翠色浓，　Endless river flows, the riverbanks are green
扁舟离离送千峰。　My skiff drifts accompanied by thousand hill.
醉里偏怜江水绿，　When drunken I fall in love with the waters
意中已想霜叶红。　In sleep I dream of the marble-covered fall.

大宁河·巴雾峡
Daning River　Bawu Gorge

神思
Pondering

波光粼粼
Ripples

巫峡深处
In the Depths of Wu Gorge

马归山
Horse-returning Hill

栩栩如生的马归山，马的前半部分隐于岩石之内，马肚、马屁股、马尾悬于外。不知者定以为是哪位雕塑名家的杰作，谁也想不到这一人间绝景竟是天造地设!

诗云："骅骝归山去，尔尾尚露天。"

The lifelike Horse-returning Mountain shapes like a horse . The front part of a horse hides among the rocks. Horse's stomach, ass, tail hang outside. The traveller may believe that it's a famous sculpter's work, yet it's the creation of the God . There is a poem praising it-the stallion the hill cannot confine, yet, its dangling tail lies in the half sky .

飞翠
Green

船动湖光滟滟秋
Sailing Boats, Lake and Autumn

两岸猿声啼不住，
轻舟已过万重山。

With monkeys' sad adieus the riverbank are loud,
My skiff has left ten thousand mountains far away.

巫山小三峡
The Lesser Three Gorge

百舸争流
Hundred Boats Swarm

白龙过江
The White Dragon Crossing the River

滴翠峡里翠欲滴，
夹岸猿声二三啼。
一叶扁舟轻波上，
修竹含情向江里。

At Emerald Gorge the landscape attracts you more,
Two or three monkeys' adieus echo the rivershore.
My skiff moves upward the streams at peace,
The bamboos tower the waters at ease.

滴翠峡
Dicui Gorge

西陵峡位于三峡东段，西起秭归县香溪河口，东至宜昌南津关，全长105公里。

西陵峡是三峡中最长的一个峡，以奇丽韶秀著称。春天，猿鸣莺啼，花絮轻扬；秋季，枫林如火，漫山橘红。西陵峡又以滩多水急闻名，险滩处，水流如沸，激荡汹涌，惊险万状。几十年来，西陵峡河道有了很大改善，特别是葛洲坝电站修建后，上游水位普遍提高。人们再无返舟之险，而又增加了峡谷寻幽的情趣。

Elegant Xiling Gorge

Xiling Gorge is situated in the eastern section of the Three Gorges, starting from the mouth of Fragrance Brook of Zigui county, in the west ends at Nanjin Pass of Yichang City in the east. It covers a long distance fo 105 km.

Xiling Gorge is one of the longest part in the Three Gorge, and famous for its gracefulness. Within the gorge, monkeys howl, orioles sing and the flowers fly in spring. The marple leaves look reddish and the orange trees scatter around the mountain in autumn. It's also renowned as many shoals and rapids. At dangerous shoals, the water surges violently like the boiling water, and full of danger. In the past decades, the waterway has been changed greatly, especially after the completion of the Project, the water level in the upper reach has been raised, People now have no risk of travelling here, but have more pleasures when sightseeing here.

西陵峡は湖北省、秭帰県の香渓河口から宜昌市の南津関まで、全長105kmであり、一番長い峡谷である。両岸の山岩には穴がいくつ開いている風箱峡や、牛の肝臓に似る怪石が懸けている牛肝馬肺峡や、山の頂上に4つの岩が水面に倒影された灯影峡などの奇岩怪石は黄濁した流水を挟んでいるようであり、河の水が時には渦巻き、泡立っていて、暗礁の上を激しく流れていく。とりわけ名高い青灘、洩灘など多くの難所になっている。三峡水利電力プロジェクトダムは間もなくここに現れる。

西陵之秋
Autumn of Xiling Gorge

金波唱晚
Golden Waves Welcome the Returing Boats

一片斜阳醉晚枫
a Ray of Sunset Glow on Marples

独钓
Fishing Lonely

西陵北沱
Beituo at Xiling Gorge

仙人桥
Fairy Bridge

九龙奔江
Nine Dragons Roaring into the River

春意
Breezy Spring

桃花依旧
Peach in Blossom

峡江日暮
Dusk at the River

灯影峡
Light Shadow Gorge

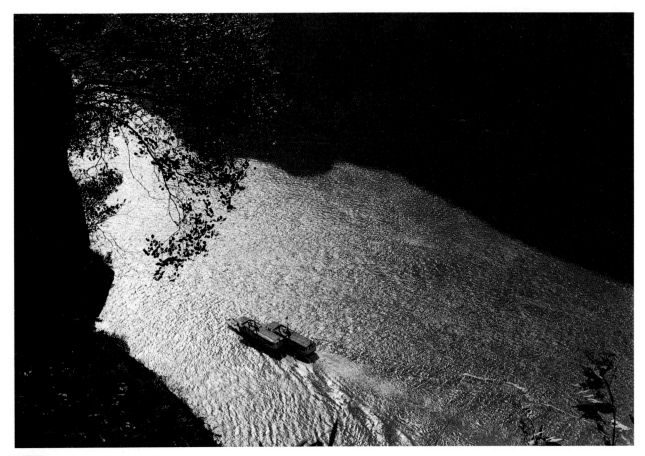

西陵深谷
Deep Valley at Xiling Gorge

崆岭晚归
Returning Boats at Kongling Gorge

崆岭绝壁
Steep Cliffs at Kongling

聚鱼坊
Fish-collection Street

At Mount Wu twelve peaks linger,
In deep valley thousand cliffs mingle.
The river flows as a running cloud pass by,
I can't tell the distant hills from the neighboring trees beneath the sky.

巫山连绵十二峰，
万仞皆在碧虚中。
江流回合云藏月，
远山近树暮连空。

九畹溪
Nine-Pie Brook

聚鱼坊地处九畹溪与长江汇合处。九畹溪保持了"玻璃澈底镜面平"的清亮水色。纯净的溪水与浑黄的江水形成"泾渭分明"的锦水奇观。

The Fish-collection Village lies at the meeting point between Nine Pie Brook and Yangtze River. Nine Pie Brook enjoys the reputation of "mirrorlike surface with glassy bottom". The clean water and roaring Yangtze River form a peculiar view.

红叶
Red Leave

修竹依依　Drooping bamboo

要留下恬静、淡泊、要　　　　　Tranquil, peaceful,
留下时光暗暗的擦痕　　　　　　Hazy scraps of timo,
一叶孤舟，一种怡然的心境呵　　A lonely skiff, a contented mood,
微风泛起的波澜里，流逝的　　　In the ripples, in the breeze
人生在寂寞的生活中还原　　　　The elapsed life imposes a promised
到了一个澄明的梦呓　　　　　　Dream upon our lonely life.

兵书宝剑峡
Tactic Books and Sword Gorge

　　"兵书宝剑"位于长江北岸，峭壁上有一叠层次分明的岩石，形似书卷堆放，人称"兵书"。在兵书的侧面，有一块石头，形如宝剑，插入江中，即所谓"宝剑"。相传诸葛亮晚年时，将平生用兵之计写成一部兵书，因蜀中无人可授，又恐落入乱臣手中，故将兵书宝剑藏于大峡之中，让后世勇士取拿。天长日久，兵书和宝剑就化作了岩石。

　　Tactic Books and Sword on the top of a north bank cliff is a stack of rock slabs that resemble a pile of books, called "tactics books", and a sword-shaped rock on one side, which is thrust in the river, referred to as "sword". The legend goes that Zhuge Liang, in his remaining years, wrote books of tactics he had used in all of his military life. As there was no one in Shu (his native place, a kingdom then) so gifted as to be able to learn his tactics and as Zhuge wanted to keep the books out of the reach of the treacherous court officials, he ended up hiding the books and his sword in the gorge for valiant people of later ages to find. The books and the sword, however, have turned into stone with the passage of time.

宝剑
Sword

兵书
Tactic Books

牛肝马肺峡
Ox Liver and Horse Lung Gorge

牛肝
Ox Liver

马肺
Horse Lung

　　牛肝马肺峡位于新滩、崆岭之间，峡中峭壁对峙，奇峰环拱。北岸石壁上有两块突出下垂的岩石，东侧一块颜色深红，状如牛肝；西侧一块，状如马肺，故名"牛肝马肺峡"。如今，牛肝保存完好，马肺已剥落大半。据说是清光绪年间，被英军舰开炮轰击所致。

　　The Ox Liver and Horse Lung Gorge lies between Xintan Shoal and kongling Gorge. Two other rocks hang overlapping from the sheer cliff on the north bank. The one in the east appears red, like an ox liver; and the other a horse lung. Hence It's name. Now, Ox Liver is preserved perfectly, but Horse lung is almost damaged. It says that it was damaged by the cannon fire from British fleets in Qing Dynasty.

崆岭峡
Kongling Gorge

西陵破晓   *Day-Break at Xiling Gorge*

在轻烟薄雾的黎明，
空自漂泊的人生的木船向生命更深处溯游，
不要说我们不曾对命运跪伏地低呵在它的敞开、
包容和接纳里一个如诗如画的世界在时光中变得更
加深邃
At thin-misted dawn,
The wandering boat sail to the deep of life.
Don't say that we don't bow to fate,
In our pray,

飞来庙　Feilai Temple

西陵小新滩

春花三月峡江清，
两岸风光喜煞人。
叠嶂层峦披翠绿，
山歌对唱尽欢声。

At March, the spring flowers along the Gorge River are seen,
Landscape on the river shore is attractive all the way.
Piles and layers of mountaintops covered with green,
All the mountains and stream water sing happily for the spring.

春

千里莺啼绿映红，
桃枝山影沐江风。
江峡逶迤三百里，
几多神话遁水中。

The oriole sings among the riverbanks and hills,
Peach branches and mountain shadows drawn in the breeze,
Gorges and streams linger for three hundred miles,
Tremendous fairy tales have poured into the isles.

青山垂练
The Falling Water

春 Spring

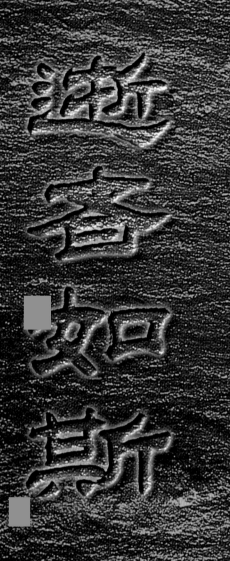

长江三峡，风情无限！古往今来，三峡荟萃了众多的文人墨客。千百年来，峡江人民在这里创造了灿烂的巴楚文明。

随着三峡水利枢纽工程的建设，水位的提高，三峡景观会发生较大的变化。许多珍贵的人文景观和风光名胜将淹没在浩淼的江波之下。例如：峡江纤夫。他们祖祖辈辈在逆流中搏搏，两岸留下他们的足迹。这是我们民族的脊梁，是中华民族苦难的脚印！逝者如斯，我们不得不在这些珍贵的遗迹而叹息，拖腕！

Gone with the water

How attractive the Three Gorges are!

From the ancient times. It had attracted a number of famous poets and men of letters, and the natives living here had created splendid Bachu Civilization.

With the Construction of Three Gorge Hydraulic Pivot Project and the raising of the water level, the landscapes here will be changed fantastically. Many valuable scenic spots and historic interests will be buried under the violent water. Take the boat trackers for example, they had been struggling against the current from generation to generation and landing their feet on the either banks. They're the backbones of our nation, and also a symbol of suffering! Gone with the water! we have to sigh, feel pitiful facing such buried valuable, relics!

長江三峡の美しい自然風景と何千年ほどの人文景観は三峡工程ダムの竣工に連れて永遠に水の底に沈まれてしまう。現代文明は昔日の輝きを取替え、しかも発展させるのは歴史の必然であるが、それとともに無限の遺憾をもわれわれの心に刻まれている。最後の最後に、三峡を楽しめよう。

韧 (奉节, 1990.6)
Boat Trackers Pulling against currents

搏(1990.6)
Struggling

石痕(香炉滩，1994.5)
Rock Tails

千百年来，纤夫赤身裸体，把纤绳嵌进脊梁里拉
船逆流而上，纤绳在石壁上滑行。日久，纤绳把坚硬
的石头磨擦出这样深深的痕迹。

For centuries the naked boat trackers, with
the ropes on the back, pulled the ships against
the current. As time goes on, the boat ropes
have left deep trailers on the rocks.

纤夫在绝壁上拉纤牵船。无路可行时，把石壁凿
出石阶踏脚，纤夫成年累月在这纤夫路上贴地爬行。

The boat trackers walked on the steep cliffs,
drawing the boats.

When there was no way, they welled many
stone steps on the rocks. They had been laboring
at this pathway for years.

纤夫的路(1994.9)
Pathway

古镇石板路(1990.10)
Stone Street

山(1990.10)

Hills

山民的色彩(秭归集市 1996.6)
The Colorful Life at Fair

冬痕(1993.12)
Winter

庇荫(秭归县牛口镇范家坪，1993.6)
Longlife Trees at Fanjia Village, Bull Mouth Town, Zigui County

古树何巍然，盘根不计年，
攀根依日月，拔地壮河山，
老干潜龙护，高枝蓉鹤眠，
森然将军树，神异永流传。

O! How towering the
 lifelong tree seems!
Winding roots refuse to
know the years on earth.
The branch climbs high
 with the rise of the sun.
Its shade glorifies the
waters and land.
An unkown dragon circles
round the old trunk.
And at top leaves sleeps
 an evening crane.
The trees stands there
gloomily like a general.
Its legendary tales are
repeated forever!

桐花飘香(木鱼寨，1993.6)
Fragrant Flowers at Wooden Fish Village

在峡江有制作面谱的传统手艺。傩戴这种面具有祈神、降福、驱邪、避灾的作用。

这一带还有一种带上面具，开坛唱戏的剧种叫做"傩戏"。

At Gorge region, it has been a long tradition to make masks. Wearing the mask can prevent the devils, avoid the bad luck ,pray for the god's blessings.

There exists a kind of opera called"Nuo Opera"characteristic of wearing the mask.

面谱老艺人(1985.10)
Handcraftman

金盔银甲峡
Jinkuiyinjia Gorge

锦(1978.8)
Silky Water

远古时，巴楚人的洞穴阴暗潮湿，并时常受到野兽的袭击，神农氏教人们在峡江两岸搭起了吊脚楼。如今的吊脚楼更朴实、端庄。

In the ancient time, the holes occupied by the Baschu natives were dark and damp and under attacks by the unknown breasts. Shenlong Shi (the tribe leader) taught the natives to build the hung houses on the banks of the river. Now, the hung houses looks more classical and attractive.

土家吊脚楼(鄂西，1980.8)
Hung House OF Tu Nationality

稀归上孝村(1989.7)
Shangxiao Village, Zigui

巫峡青石(1993.5)
Green Stone of Wu Gorge

聚鱼坊，临峡古建(1996 年 5 月因移民而拆除)(1984.5)
The Ancient Architecture at Fish-collection Village(detached because
of immigration in May.1996)

五月榴花照眼明(巫峡青石，1993.5)
May Flower Shining in the River (Green Stone of Wu Gorge)

在这斑驳的明清古宅里，有四个像榴花绽放般的姑娘。年年岁岁花开花谢，岁岁年年沧海桑田。三峡移民后，人去宅空，独有悠悠江水映榴花。

最后一瞥(秭归上孝村，1993.5)
The Last Glimplse